Dreams My Father Sold Me

Poems and Graphic Art of Nabil Shaban

SIRIUS BOOK WORKS publishing

For **Mordechai Vanunu**,
an Israeli hero of the late 20th century,
cruelly persecuted by his country
for exposing Israel's clandestine and illegal nuclear weapons industry
and for wanting a Nuclear Free Middle East.

I also dedicate this book to **Marcela Mikulenkova**, my Fire Horse,
who insisted that "Dreams My Father Sold Me" be published.

Cover Illustrations

Front - *Don't Blame Eve*   *Nabil Shaban 1982*
Back - *Ribbon Trip*   *Nabil Shaban 1996*

Published by Sirius Book Works publishing
84 Longacre
ASH
Nr. Aldershot
Hants GU12 6RP

First published in the United Kingdom 2005

Printed and bound in Ireland by βetaprint of Dublin

ISBN 0954829409

Nabil Shaban was born in 1953 in Amman, Jordan and arrived in England when he was three for treatment for his osteogenesis imperfecta (brittle-bone disease). In 1980, he and Richard Tomlinson founded **Graeae** (pronounced Grey Eye), a professional theatre company of disabled performers. A writer and performer with many film and television credits, he is probably best known to television viewers for his role as ruthless intergalactic businessman Sil in the *Doctor Who* stories **'Vengeance on Varos'** and **'Trial of a Timelord'** (BBC, 1985 + 1986).

On stage he has played Volpone, Hamlet, Jesus in **Godspell**, Haille Sellassie in **'The Emperor** and Ayatollah Khomeini in **Iranian Nights**, Mack the Knife in Theatre Workshop's production of Brecht's "**Threepenny Opera**"

He also played the storyteller Rashid in the Royal National Theatre's production of Salman Rushdie's "**Haroun and the Sea of Stories**".

He has appeared in such movies as **City of Joy** (d. Roland Joffe, 1991), **Wittgenstein** (d. Derek Jarman, 1992) and **Born of Fire** (d. Jamil Dehlavi, 1988), and on television in **Walter** and **Deptford Graffiti**.

Nabil Shaban is a political actor and has worked in plays about Palestine (**The Little Lamp**, 1999 and **Jasmine Road**, 2003), about the State murder of Northern Ireland lawyer, Rosemary Nelson (**Portadown Blues**, 2000). Also "**D.A.R.E.**" (disabled terrorists opposed to genetic cleansing of disabled people) (1997-2004).

Shaban has written and presented several documentaries on themes of disability, including the Emmy award winning **Skin Horse** (Channel 4, 1983), about disability and sexuality, the **Fifth Gospel** (BBC, 1990), exploring the relationship between the Christianity and disability. He also instigated and presented the Without Walls: **'Supercrips and Rejects'** (Channel 4, 1996), about Hollywood's representation of disabled people. Also in a Secret History documentary "**The Strangest Viking**" (Channel 4, 2003), he argued the case that Ivarr the Boneless was a disabled viking leader.

In 1995, he founded *Sirius Pictures* to make video arts documentary **Another World**. This was followed in 1997 by **'The Alien Who Lived in Sheds'** (BBC, 1997) which he wrote, directed and starred in..

Shaban's written plays include "**The First To Go**" (about disabled people in Germany's Third Reich) and "**I am the Walrus**" (about a schizophrenic who believes he made Mark Chapman assassinate John Lennon)

Nabil Shaban, who has a degree in Psychology and Philosophy, was awarded in 1997 an honorary doctorate from the University of Surrey for the achievements of his career and his work to change public perceptions of disabled people.

---CONTENTS----

PICTURES

POEMS

PICTURES

POEMS

FOREWORD
by Lord Richard Attenborough

Towards the end of the 18th Century, Edward Burke made the statement "All that is necessary for the triumph of evil is that good men do nothing". He need have had no fears as far as Nabil Shaban is concerned. He is a remarkable man, talented, committed and tireless in pursuit of what he believes. He is also uncompromisingly courageous. In some degree the world has not been kind to him. He is, however, undaunted in that he was involved in the creation of Graeae which, of course, proved to be a triumphantly successful concept. Opportunities should properly be accessible for anyone wishing to express themselves in artistic terms and Graeae has unquestionably proved this possible. The great thing about Nabil, however, is that he has helped to further that conviction for so many.

This magical book is fascinating evidence of his skills, not only as a poet, but also as a draughtsman. He is to be admired and congratulated on both accounts.

INTRODUCTION
by Colin Baker

I worked with Nabil Shaban in 1984. He astonished us all when, at the read through of Vengeance on Varos - a Doctor Who story, he produced a chilling and witty characterisation of the larva-like alien, Sil. He created an ululating and wicked laugh that many since have tried to emulate without success. John Nathan Turner the series' producer was quick to realise the originality and success of Nabil's character and commissioned a script that included Sil for the next season. Nabil's personal story is his own to tell, but suffice it to say that he has not been deterred from living his life to the full by an introduction to the world that might have banished hope from all but the strongest individual. Nabil proves the old dictum "There are no obstacles, just opportunities."

His writings and artwork are very personal and offer an illuminating insight into the life, worldview and mindset of their creator. "Is it a Prophecy?" and "The Headless Man" both written around the time that Nabil, the actor, was delighting both the cast and the worldwide audience of Doctor Who, are prime and poignant examples of his view of his own (and our) place in a world torn apart by personal and political strife. "Hitler is not Dead" and "Alienation" should be read by every "able bodied" person to gain a glimpse of what it must be like to inhabit a body that has the potential to limit ambition, even though Nabil himself has never succumbed to that easy option.

The very use of the word "sold" rather than "gave" in the title of this direct and stark anthology tells us as much as the words he has written, as does the haunting image of the silhouetted figure (Nabil / Sil?) in the wheelchair, gazing over a calm expanse of water, perched on smooth rocks from below which peer hooded and malevolent eyes.

For all the above reasons and because he is a great bloke - I commend "Dreams my Father Sold Me" to you.

Author's Introduction

I hated poetry when I was at school. I hated reading it...reciting it...writing it. Our English teacher was a real bully. A real genius for creating new reasons for beating us. The Torture of Poetry Recit-tititi-tation was his next sad invention. We had to learn a new poem every week. He always chose the longest and most difficult ones for us to learn off by heart. We were given the damned poem on Monday and we had to know it word perfect by Friday afternoon...and woe betide anyone who forgot a single syllable or mumbled or stumbled over any line. You got the broomstick across your arse or ruler on your hand...or in my case my head got walloped with a hefty volume of the Encyclopedia Brittanica. But I was very stubborn and simply went on strike. Refused point blank to cooperate. It was a battle of wills between me and the poetry tyrant. Every Friday for a month, he would ask me if I had learned the poem set on Monday and I would defiantly say "NO, not a word - SIR". Well, it just seemed a pointless exercise. What were we? Performing parrots? Anyway, it didn't matter how much I tried to reason with SIR, it would still end up me getting another battering on the poor old bonce. I'm sure that's why I stayed small. Repeated hammerings with heavy books of knowledge must have stunted my growth. It was "Ozymandias - king of kings" who finally broke the regime. For three weeks I refused to learn that poem. And in the end because of the bad example I was setting (other pupils were beginning to resist like me) the teacher dropped the whole miserable exercise of trying to instil a robotic mindless love of the great English "poemists". I had won a small victory but in the end you could say he had the last laugh because here I am publishing my first book and it's a bloody book of poetry. Who would have thought it possible.

India. November 1983. Having a refreshing cleansing shower in a hotel room in Calcutta... That's when the Muse took her revenge.. Suddenly a dream came back to me. Or rather the lines of a song from a dream I'd had the previous night. "If you walk in my dreams, my dear....". I wanted to hear the rest of the song, so I had to make it up . Then, as I continued to feel the warm relaxing waters cascade upon me, I slipped into another rhyming reverie and began to improvise another song "Take me back to the River...." Thus, the Muse amused herself by infecting me with the desire to create poetry. And for the next 20 years the spaghetti words wormed their way out of my upper orifice.

As for painting. Making pictures. That compulsion began much earlier. I'd noticed that boys who were good at drawing, always seemed to attract the girls. I was nine at the time. Okay, so I was a sex maniac at an early age. I'd discovered that a lot of girls love horses, so I attempted to woo my first girl with a scratchy sketch of a rearing fiery horse. She was not impressed. So I donated the picture to the X-ray department in the local hospital. It was a "Thank You" present. I had broken my arm (again) and the lady radiologist had been very gentle and I had fallen in love with her. I was still only nine.

....And that's it. There's nothing more for me to say about this my first book, "Dreams My father Sold Me". I'll just let the words and pictures speak for themselves. And if they seem strangely silent then feel free to give them your voice.

18:53, 30th August 2004

"Whoever did that painting, should see a psychiatrist"
                              -    George

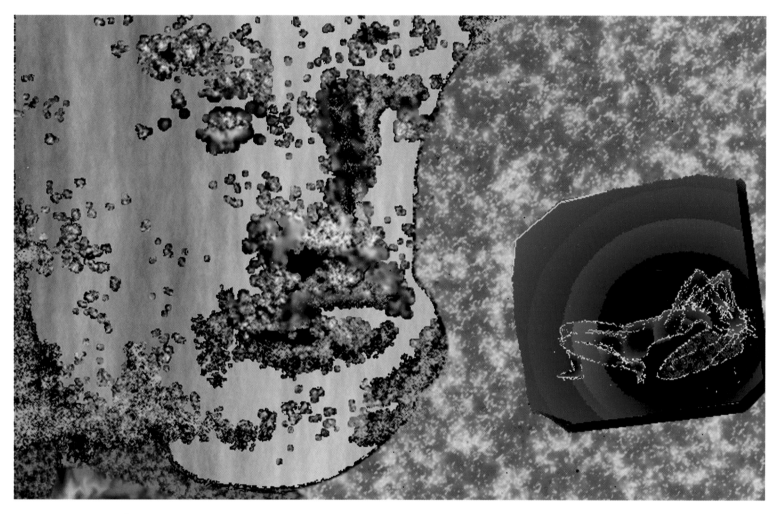

LSD Fairy Throws a Crumbling Dice   Nabil Shaban 1996

Walk in My Dreams

If you walk in my dreams my dear,
You'll see you have nothing to fear,
We won't be sucked into Silly Cloud Nine,
You'll realise my mind you won't mind.
Dark mysteries, shining hope and pure love,
Are the things I try to dream of,
But I need a partner to dispel,
My weakness for this material Hell.

If you walk in my dreams my dear,
We'll emerge in a world so clear,
And if you let me walk in your own,
I know I'll have found my lost home,
So don't pretend you don't know me,
We met when we were both lonely,
Our knowing looks caught in aspic,
The card you dealt was my last trick.

12th December 1983

Stone Axis   Nabil Shaban 1998

Don't Crawl Up the Volcano.

Take me back to the River,
To the one that's hard to Cross,
I want a boat without a sail,
Now that my life is All but Lost.

Chorus:
Don't crawl up the Volcano,
It's not as steep as it seems,
The inferno within is no match,
To begin the power of your dreams.

There's a Man way up the River,
And He's got my name in His hands,
Through His fingers it drips away,
Like the eternal shifting sands.

The stars are falling around me,
I'm trying to shelter my head,
But my hands wave to set me free,
They'd sooner fly than souls go dead.

Somewhere there's a Glass Rainbow,
In a case of molten lead,
And a key that's meant for turning,
In a belly that's starved of bread.

Take me back to the River,
I can't swim, but I'll never drown,
I want to live like a Saviour,
But I've dreams, not thorns for a crown.

12th December 1983

Web Wyrd

Nabil Shaban 1999

Look at Me.

When you're looking, looking at me,
What do you see? What do you see?
Is it Fact? Or pure Fantasy?
Or a strange mixture of all Three?

Am I great or am I small?
Does my smile make me seem tall?
If they gave you one small wish,
Would I be changed for a tastier dish?

Tell me, is my nose out of place?
Should it be elsewhere, not on my face?
Are my bizarre looks in the way?
Do they obscure my soul at play?

Do you see me as imperfect?
Or is my query incorrect?
Should I accept your good intent?
Not think your love is somewhat bent?

25th February 1984

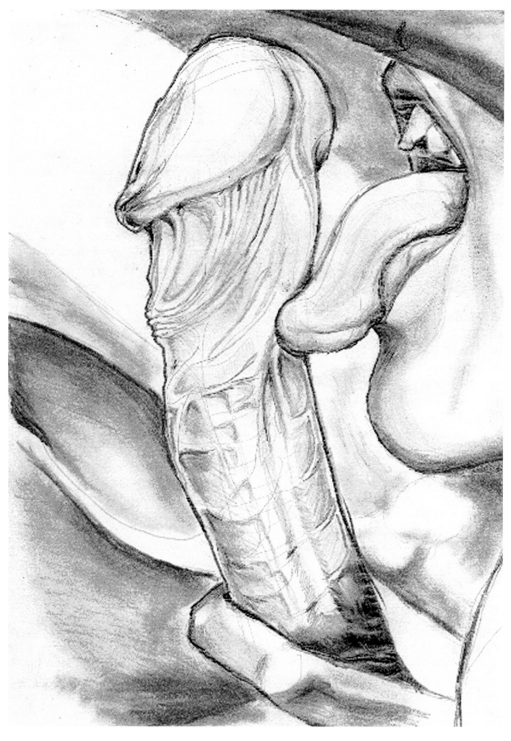

Iguana Dance from Mars   Nabil Shaban 1983

The Ballad of the Sex War.

The only thing he's thinking , he must screw Julie.
Her Holy Hole is shrinking - it must be filled truely,
Her Loving Cup he's drinking - gulping so unruely,
In her anus his finger inserted,
As it wiggles, she thinks he's perverted,
But she adores it all the same,
And begs him to do it again.

As their lips fasten together,
She whips his arse with leather,
As the blood bursts from his weals,
She adds hurt with stilletto heels.
As the sweat begins to pour,
He screams out names like "Bitch", "Whore".

In her mouth his cock sucked sore,
Until he begs "Please, no more!"
But his balls are in her hands,
Grinding them 'til strands.
As he whimpers out his last breath,
She gloats "Mere holes can't inflict Death."

22nd March 1984

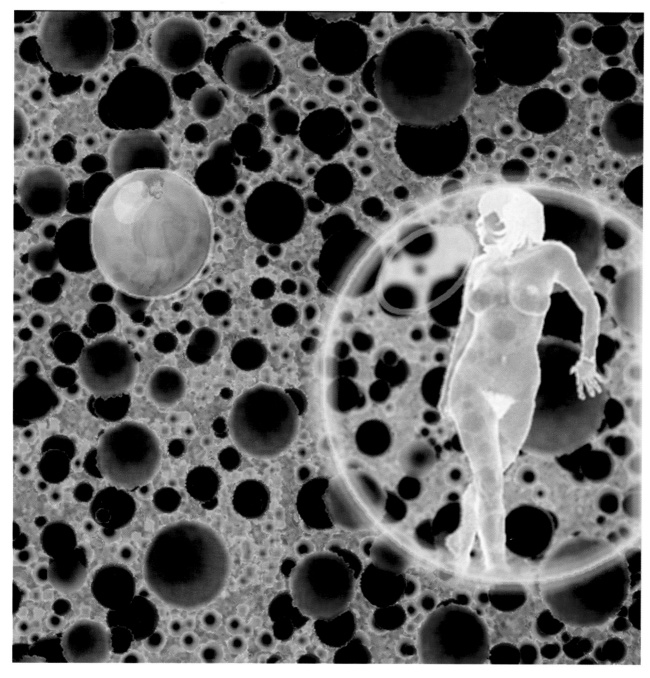

Sphear   Nabil Shaban   1998

Nagging Doubts

Baby, it's cool when you take me to school,
You do teach me how to use this young tool,
But the angels cry, "This is all a lie!
If you fuck without love, your soul will die!"
May be it's all true but what can I do
When this vision of you beckons me - SCREW!

Oh God, let me die if to live I must lie,
That's not what I want, to drink lust at her font.

She awoke the Kraken within,
They all spoke of the Maker of Sin,
Now I know what it was I was missing,
It's something much more than just kissing,
Is it only sex that now turns my head?
Are women just holes to be screwed and bled?

Don't let it be said I just live for her bed
I know she wants more of us men than menace.

23rd March 1984

InterFractAisle Twist   Nabil Shaban 2001

Down The Pan

The rose petal penetrates to a cavernous deep,
Light-fingeredly falling on the soft sheen of her sleep,
Murmuring, simmering, the eye of her sigh awakes,
But not soon enough - for, her virginity he breaks,
"Out!" was her cry, and forced him upwards to the ceiling,
But to the floor down she fell, her maidenhood reeling,
Hurriedly through the window the thief went, his seed woe spent,
Leaving behind something unkind - a woman for rent,
Leaving behind an unwanted child in foment,
Leaving behind a once blooming life....in cement.

24th March 1984

Swept by a New Bloom   Nabil Shaban 1999

Know Thyself

I am the Way, the Life and the Truth,
But I am getting long in the tooth.
    I am the Rock, the Light and the Door,
    But I can't save souls anymore.

I am the Truth, the Way and the Life,
Please help me, I can't stop all this strife.
    I am the Door, the Light and the Rock,
    I may have failed but...Love - Don't knock.

I am the Life, the Truth and the Way,
Dead may be, but I'll live if you pray.
    I am the Door, the Rock and the Light,
    But it will be Alright on the Night.

26th March 1984

The Journey is the Thing   Nabil Shaban 1984

RARNROURK

Rarnrourk on the side of Moon-tide,
Rarnrourk in the House of Past-died,
Rarnrourk running at the Fast-end,
Rarnrourk having to now pretend.

Show me the Sign at the end of the Line,
Show me the Hope at the end of the 'Scope,
Show me the Home at the end of the Roam,
Show me the Sun at the end of the Run,
Show me the Light at the end of the Fight,
Show me the Death at the end of your Breath.

Rarnrourk, I can feel your claws in me,
Under your wings I shelter from thee.

Rarnrourk, crush me to your iron core,
Gripped in the fangs of your lion's jaw.

Rarnrourk, am I stuck to your soft web,
Or is my attachment to your bed?

Rarnrourk, am I imprisoned in your bee-hive,
Or will I escape intact or alive?

Climb onto the Apex where the Ape Pecks,
Fall down to Polygon where Polly's Gone,
The Eye in mid-stream floats in the missed dream,
The Base is the place where Square is the space,
On which Rarnrourk arose to lift me across,
The Abyss on Her back as the saved are lost.

29th March 1984

Recharging Towers of Silence   Nabil Shaban 2000

If I Decide

If I decide to commit suicide
How shall I do it?   ......With blade or with bleach?
Where shall I do it? .....In the glade or on beach?
Why shall I do it? ....Am I alien or a leech?

I'm closed up. No access. Me they can't reach.

If I decide to commit suicide
When shall I do it? .....Before or after the laughter?

Time blows up. "Oh!" Max says. Me they can't teach.

If I decide to commit suicide
Will I change my mind before or after I die?

3rd April 1984

Go away, you've come to the wrong place   Nabil Shaban   2002

Is it a Prophecy?

Once there was a night,
Where a dream gave fright,
Describing the End,
Of all Life could send.

"Why send me," I cry,
"This vision of Doom,
I'm only knee-high,
And fresh from the womb."

To this day not sure,
If some films I saw,
Disrupted my sleep,
With false signs to keep,
Or whether it's true,
This dream I tell you,
Warns of Things to Come,
If we all stay dumb.

This night-mirrored myth,
Your mind shall I fill,
Of a world short-lived,
Haunts me, taunts me still.

Cliffs of plunging wrath,
Rips the earth gone soft,
On heat cracks emerge,
From cities crowds surge,
Alone. Unloved. Lost.
Trapped by flame and frost,
The War-lords' machine,
Mega-deaths they breath,
To make the world clean,
But what did they leave?

Man's science gone mad,
Now, Nature's turned bad,
The despair sets in,
No return from sin,
Destinies squandered,
"How?" to be pondered,
Not by Man now past,
But insects and grass.

Is it really true,
No more me or you?

23rd May 1984

Yank Entertainment   Nabil Shaban 2004

No Turning Back

part one

The jungle was mellow, the jungle was deep,
The mist spiralling upwards like snakes on heat,
Village huts like haystacks uncluttered in sleep,
False dawn approaches when we sort chaff from wheat.

Day One of our rescue, they thought we were friends,
White forces of freedom, we land in thousands,
When, too late, they see they're the means to our ends,
And now they fly from us, no gifts can rouse tens.

The jungle was yellow, the jungle was mean,
The fist spiralling upwards like snakes in grief.

But today I don't see it, I feel secure,
Lost in Paradise, I swallow manure,
The Darkies and Gooks are a pathetic threat,
That's what they try tell us back on the film set,
So it's a joke, a hoot, a gas and a laugh,
Never us to be soaked in the coming blood bath,
Be calm, enjoy life, there's a war on, you know,
These guerillas aren't winners, it's all just show.

But as the sun creeps higher, I sweat in doubt,
Are we really the boys who carry the clout?
We take it on trust only bad guys drop dead,
Who are we fighting, sir, no one has yet said?
It's rumoured the V.C. but I don't agree,
That war was over by the year 'Seventy-three,
And even more crazy, some say it's the Jap,
But he stopped fighting after our Atom crap,
"Who then, the Chinese?", I tentatively put,
"Don't be daft", they laughed, "Up Bear arse Chink's foot."

The jungle was yellow, the jungle was mean,
The fist spiralling upwards like snakes in grief.
So it's a joke, a hoot, a gas and a laugh,
Never us to be soaked in the coming blood bath.

No one will tell me. They probably don't know,
Who cares now the Enemy aint far to go,
Advancing, pushing, like ghost-cats in the dark,
To encircle us with their sinister psyche,
Riding their bicycles, eating their ricey.

Soldier, Soldier, will you Marry Me   Nabil Shaban   2003

No quarter, no prisoners, that's war today,
Rules of Genghiz are in vogue again, you say,
These people mean business, each one's a hero,
Fighting for new life, the old was worth zero

While we regimental puppets gone soft,
With brass buttons, not ideals, covered in spots,
And jokers who laugh when cooking natives' feet,
And trying to shoot the Colonel's parrokeet,
And poets should never be fighting in wars,
Where confusion abounds and greyness clouds cause.

The jungle was yellow, the jungle was mean,
The fist spiralling upwards like snakes in grief.
So it's a joke, a hoot, a gas and a laugh,
Never us to be soaked in the coming blood bath.

It's only now I care with death in the air,
I was keen to enlist...or was is a dare?
Now it don't matter, too late for reasons why,
It all comes to the same thing when I must die.

Part two

Now I know why there's this quake in my heart,
Twas a dream this morning that gave me a start,
The guarded air was sliced by a woman's scream,
On waking, turned into split figs in the stream.

Quaking dreams shift to split figs in the stream.

Reassured, I made haste to the man in charge,
Who ordered me to take grave news to the Sarge,
Dropped like a coconut on a Dodo's egg,
Evacuate and burn, ignore if they beg,
Evacuate and burn, shoot if they beg,
Denigrate concern, deplore the weaks' ache.

Quaking dreams shift to slit pigs in mint cream.

Collateral Damage? Turkey Shoot? Bug Splat? Who Cares, Anyway   Nabil Shaban 2004

The panic that ensued caused a bloody mess,
Spooked chickens without heads couldn't have done worse,
We think we're on TV, and death ain't real,
The men goose the women and have their last feel,
And the women prance, making face-packs of mud,
At least lipstick and rouge will help hide the blood,
I watch the chaos as they fling flames at all,
The proof that for most of us the end must fall.

The jungle was hell on earth, the jungle was obscene,
The shit spiralling downwards like cakes in spit.

So it's a joke, a hoot, a gas and a laugh,
Never us to be soaked in the coming blood bath.

We wait for the Choppers, our only escape,
They can't land, we must climb ropes as thin as thread,
The other bad news, not enough craft to go round,
And not allowed to return, once homeward bound.

I grabbed the Colonel by the scum of the neck,
And screamed, "Tell WHY, or I'll rub you into flem!",
"Time's running short and we've got to win this war,
Not by conventional forces any more,
The plan is to Nuke the whole population,
This has been agreed by more than one nation,
And any one Left by a quarter to three,
Must say a prayer and hang themselves from THAT tree!"

Quaking dreams shift to sick digs in extreme.

"Does that include you?" I stunk out with crammed hate,
"I don't know?" It now depends on you my fate!"
At this I released this squirming Life-Robber,
And helped him aboard the last Hell-Hopper,
And as he and his crew disappear from view,
I knew, as a victim my freedom was true,
I've found my peace being martyred with the weak,
Rather this than be part of crimes born of spiteful pique.

The jungle was hollow, the jungle full of sheep,
The kiss towering above us like Shakespeare's teeth.
So it's a joke, a hoot, a gas and a laugh,
Never us to be soaked in the coming blood baa baa BAA BATH.

"I am Become Death"   Nabil Shaban 2004

part three

It's now gone three and I'm waiting, still unhung,
I'm not swinging to death's tune until it's sung,
Never us to be croaked in the damming dud art,
Numbing Mum's part, fanning Dad's nark.

And then I was sure my delay was not poor,
Out of the brush came a rush of troops galore,
But, damn, all hope dimmed when it became clear,
Their plight was more perished than ours out here,
"We've had it," their commanding officer sighed,
"Out there, too many of Nature's best have died."
"On both sides of the line?" I gently hinted,
She nodded "Yes", her compasion unstinted,
And then warned, "The Enemy will soon arrive",
"Who? Not even our own want us alive!"

And when I said this, an iced scream split the screen,
And awoke from a dream, the worse I've yet had....

The jungle was mellow, the jungle was mean....
The young ones were yelling, the young ones were green...

But before calm could wash, my eyes try to bleat,
I'm in a new war with it's stench of defeat,

The mist spiralling upwards like snakes on heat...
The list scrolling downwards like slaves on a leash...

Then I knew from this Dream leave I could never,
My eyelids have become stapled together.

The jungle's not mellow, the jungle's too steep,
The bliss won't creep forward 'cause snails don't cheat.

THE END....BUT NOT THE END.

23rd August 1984

41

What Have I Done?   Nabil Shaban 1986

Rock My Soul in a Rolls Royce

Rock my Soul in a Rolls Royce,
Yer got no money and yer got no choice,
Yer kick yer Ma in the teeth,
And yer Pa's a joke,
But yer got a Rocking song,
And yer going for broke.

Rock my Soul in a Rolls Royce,
Yer wanna be all hard but yer eyes go moist,
Yer body aches all over,
And yer sure to croak,
But yer got a Rocking song,
And yer going for broke.

Rock my Soul in a Rolls Royce,
Yer wanna write the filth but yer owe James Joyce,
Yer hit the bottle all day,
In the night yer smoke,
But yer got a Rocking song,
And yer going for broke.

6th Dec. 1990

Church of the Tiny Comfort

Nabil Shaban   2001

DEAD IN SEPTEMBER

If you wanna bee down in January,
You gotta go round and scare the fairy,
And then the town is bound to call your bluff,
'Cause to taunt the Lord ain't cool enough,
'Cause to haunt the Lord ain't cruel enough,
'Cause to flaunt the Lord ain't good enough.

If you wanna feel Grim in February,
You'll be out on a limb, in death be wary,
Stars will slip you a sin if you grease their grin,
Chuck the Cross in the bin, whilest God sips gin.

If you wanna bee encouraged to March,
Just bury your Art beneath the whore's Arch,
Don't count the pounds before they drown your brain,
Love at a price costs more for the insane.

If you wanna play the Ape in April,
Just wrap your face in tape 'coz looks can kill,
The Eye in the Sky loves to see you die,
And in the rush to dust, don't reason why.

If you wanna be a Mother in May,
Sigh and live death for love's paltry pay,
If you wanna be a Father too soon,
Kill the Johnnie and fill a lead balloon.

If you wanna bee a dog in June,
Just cock your trigger and spook the Moon,
Let weeping Gods cry if the powder's dry,
A barrel of laughs will make cow dung fly.

Road Movie

Nabil Shaban 1999

If you wanna have Justice in July,
Carve out a block of ice and let it fry,
The law's an ass and mustn't be obeyed,
The rich brays braver and the poor's afraid.

 If you wanna bee Awesome in August,
Jack up some crack and let your skull go bust,
Let the slime slide as you ride out your time,
Heavenly Hates will create Hell outta crime.

If you wanna bee Dead in September,
You gotta forget and not remember,
That your past is burnt on strips of leather,
You can't fall the fool from Grace forever.

If you wanna bee shot in October,
Just buy a toy gun and pray you're sober,
The pigs will have fun, they need no excuse,
Sad souls they love drilling when out of juice.

If you wanna know all in November,
Just read what they sow, but be no member,
Everything's within, don't need their sin,
They will teach, reach, burn you…Don't let them in.

If you wanna day dream in December,
Just slit your throat when drinking distemper,
Then you'll be free to paint pictures of me,
That are real and loving in harmony.

17th February 1992

He Cannot Flatter

Nabil Shaban 1997

Nice John Thomas

Time when he thought knew who he was,
Male, white, young and physically able,
Joy through Strength,
Smash the table,
The world was his,
Oysters ate from his cradle,
Boy, did he sense he couldn't lose.

Okay, his education was pretty naff, so what?
Average like the rest, maybe even less, so what?
He had the nowse, that's what matters,
If the school fails, who gives a shit?
He'll make up for it, in the army,
They'll give him a training,
Help him laugh as they kick his brain in,
Okay, a few years taking orders,
But he's no bleeding waiter,
His day won't come much later,
And he can start giving them.

He'll get to know, ho - ho,
Every bit of his body, yo - yo,
So finely tuned his control,
The minutest of utmost muscles will snap, crackle,
And how's your Father,
To attend the smart-bomb precision,
It was his decision,
If you don't believe me, just read the posters.

But, and gor blimey, it's a big butt,
None of it worked out how he thought it should,
The army didn't give a toss about him, really,
His physique and obedience, oh bee hee hee dee ents,
Was all they loved dearly,
Never officer material,
Just a polisher of leather,
Wee Wally didn't have two,
O'levels to rub together,
Well, what was the point?

Waves of Nostalgia   Nabil Shaban 1974

School didn't mean nothing to him,
A wanking waste of time,
The lessons were always boring,
Teachers never thought you could do much, anyway,
Always telling you you're as thick as bricks,
Mostly, you're out just trying to get through the day
In between being bossed about by cunting pricks.

The most important thing he learnt at the dead brat's school,
Was how to get by with the least effort possible,
Unless you're ordered,
Never go out of your way,
To break your back,
'Cause you won't get no thanks,
If your face don't fit,
And a voice that grates,
Like a bucket of shit,
Just go for the things you know best,
Real things they couldn't fuck up for you -
Booze, betting, battling and birds -
You've got all it takes to be on the make.

Of course, we and he knew too much of his thinking,
Was stinking bluff and confusion,
Nothing unusual, just a plonker's delusion,
His big problem he couldn't apply himself,
Can't stick at anything for long.
Thought the army would help hand him his discipline,
It did, of a sort but not the right sort,
Who's a Right Charlie for being Left out?
Left, Right, Left, Right, Left, Right.

Well, what's to be done for this poor little sod?
Real application comes not from God,
(He's just a stupid old fart,
Who lost His nerve on the Cross.)
But from belief in oneself,
One's right to be relevant,
But quelle elephant surprises supreme,
No one's proven that to him,
No one's told him dat ding.
Not his parents, not his school, not the army.
Doesn't know, mustn't show, oh so donut slow,
Jesus Measles! He just does not know,
He can organise his own relevance.

An Old Layne   Nabil Shaban 1974

Guess he's been told leave it to the udders,
You gotta stay rudderless,
Coz they know best,
Only relevance he udderstands,
Is living for the present,
Application, suffocation, frustration means
Living for tomorrow,
And that's a waste of time,
So don't believe that line,
Coz they just love to lie,
In a suffering nation's sorrow,
Coz they control tomorrow,
That's their preserve,
Jammy buggers! Not his.

Well, that's what they want lover-boy to believe,
Bleeding hearts shouldn't grieve,
For twats who can't achieve,
That's what his eductaion was really about,
Head alteration to accept he can't shout,
But the trouble for the rabble is the taughtuous truth,
Has a brilliant mask wrapped in cotton wool,
Thus boxing in his rebellion in a twist of lemon,
And stunting his emotions through a tv heaven.

So he tends to relate more to things of today,
Than to future and people,
What he likes is his motor-bike,
Relationships are bollocks,
Unless just bodies for his own satisfaction,
The bike he will wed, coz he's in soul control.
It aint got a mind of it's own, Thank Sod,
If women were like that, he wouldn't be on his Todd,
He does want more, but he doesn't know how,
He's trapped with his image,
Which aint of his making,
But who's gonna wake him?
Not you. If you try now,
You'll get your head kicked in.

12th February 1992

Bury My Art but Please Not Me

Nabil Shaban 2003

The Headless Man

part one

Echos scudding on a wet look floor,
A deadly deed to settle the score,
Centre stage are grouped five men in black,
Inching towards them, I fear my back,
Their whispers slink thru the misty dark,
Red circles of light bequeath their mark,
Crouched heads jerk round, a shade of squint,
They look to me for the hidden hint.

I dribble the lines like sweating cheese,
Which builds in strength, words for weaving ease,
"The world has blown far too old", I blurt,
"But it's fall from grace we could divert,
"There's this sad Man, he clones death for all,
"When humanity heeds fast his call,
"Unknown to all, except to us six,
"New life springs not, from his loinsome tricks.

"All will love him but will rue the day,
"His creed for the world leads them ash tray,
"So, my friends, before cracked bells toll late,
"Let's act now, while he's not yet great."
They nod in agreement, they cough "Yes",
They have to accept his death no less,
"Who will perform this unholy task?",
A farce to ask, the Role long past cast.

Dressed for the part, He stepped out of line,
With that smirk of his, Fate's chilling sign,
His eyes worming the truth from the grey,
For the world, down my life He must lay,
From Him, I cannot, will not, deny,
It is I who must, for Hope's sake, die.

Out there now lurks my appointed death,
At the brush stroke of my brother's breath,
Still, I'm glad, the mission has been set,
I can sleep now, Time will free my debt.

What Is To Be Done?   Nabil Shaban 1989

part two

I am found some time past on the train,
Holding on to what's left of the sane,
The cripple that's me quakes on the tracks,
Sliding chair fro and to, my nerve cracks,
Then I sense His presence down the line,
He's creeping up the vans towards mine,
Death's shadow snakes thru the corridors,
I expect no mercy, only Jaws,
After all it was me who made Him,
We both knew this Joke was no mere whim.

Suddenly bang, doors open, there He is!
Confident, in steps this Tarot's kiss,
My eyes wide, What's He got? Gun or knife?
A blade! Good. I can still save my life,
Torn in two, my will is distorted,
Creep of Thanatos, be aborted!
I know I must let the Hymn succeed,
Prevent not I, stark destiny's need.

The smiling grim beams back the blade's gleam,
When the train deranged breaks Hade's dream,
We both fall apart and to the floor,
He's lost his knife, I've got hope once more,
The Killer scrabbles and grabs His tool,
While I grip His wrists, from His lips come drool,
Fate's struggling dagger goes back and forth,
I try to push His blade back up north.

I know it's a sin. We had a deal,
He was to kill me. The world would heal,
But I can't, won't, for no one, die,
With my utmost will, I'll bleed Him dry,
Success! His eyes cry. Now glazed. Now shut,
I've forced His knife up, ripped His own gut,
I won, but I'm suffering from shock,
The world's now doomed to suck my cock.

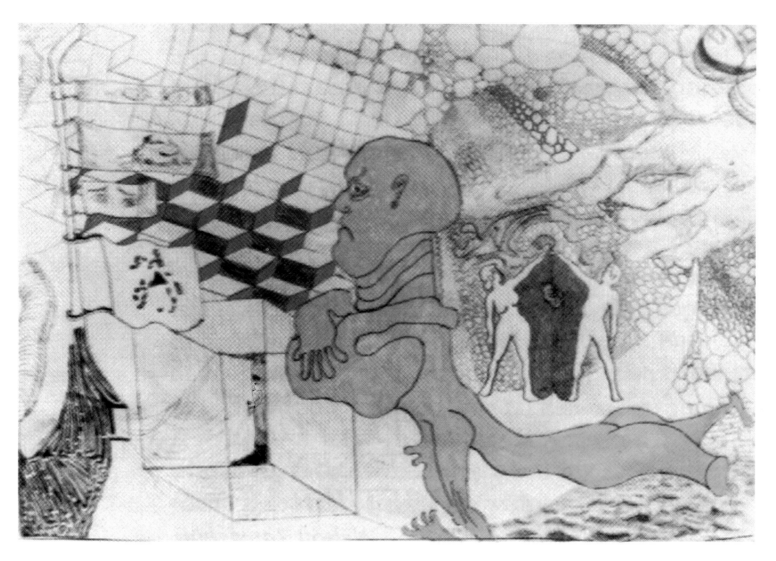

Nowhere Man   Nabil Shaban 1982

part three

Years have flown by, the nightmare's faded,
I'm near the Top, the world's been raided,
Now I can walk and stand with the tall,
With stunning good looks, I excel all,
Married to a princess, soon to be Queen,
With an envied palace, the best yet seen,
I'm a rich, powerful superstar,
No one can stop me, I've gone too far.

Much loved by the global media,
It's mine, that's why it's now seedier,
Elected Business Man of the Year,
Eminent Statesman, Mister Sincere,
The New World Order's my invention,
Created to suppress dissention,
The plebs will stay tame with bread and games,
Soon I will be World Controller of Names.

I've been praised for solving with slick ease,
Problems of famine, drought and disease,
My genius has cracked the energy gap,
Unlimited fuel, just turn the tap,
My Peace Plan has won the Nobel Prize,
Won an Oscar for "Master of Lies",
Soon they'll vote me World Ruler Supreme,
And then they'll know I'm not what I seem.

Upstairs bathroom, I'm having a shave,
My wife's adorning the silk I gave,
We're preparing for an evening out,
Dressed to kill, there are smart Gods about,
We're honoured guests at the White House ball,
Where I'll condescend to take the Call,
Tonight, Time waits for the razor blade,
Life spliced on the Edge, poised for the Shade.

Not long now for the posh sleek limo,
To pick us up for the Last Laugh Show,
But in the mirror I see no grin,
Something ominous has just crept in,
A shadowy feeling sensing doom,
This shaking shave craves blood for my tomb,
Echos return to collect lost bills,
There's a Song to be paid, one that thrills,
"Oh Razor, please Razor, cut my throat,
Time to take me on your Death-Wish boat."

The Holy Grail

Nabil Shaban 2004

Tell me I'm a Melancholy Man,
I don'tunderstand the risk I ran,
My Ego awoke God's Evil Plan,
Now He hints I must carry the can.

Ghosts never die, they're made to haunt you,
The door bell rings and I'm torn in two,
I'm still upstairs but I see the hall,
"It's okay, I'll go," comes my wife's call,
I watch her as she descends the stairs,
While a silent prickling scares my hairs,
"The chauffeur's early," she says, annoyed,
Opens the door to a black night's void.

At first, she just felt the smiling stare,
Shadows were shielding Him standing there,
So out stepped the Smile into the light,
Fate urged Him back for a second bite,
A luminous face, eyes sparkling red,
My Assassin returns from the Dead,
His quiet charm fills my wife with dread,
He's from that Place where angels can't tread.

"Who are you?" she asks fearing His voice,
He doesn't answer, He has no choice,
But to extend His benevolence,
And takes off His hat that gave offence,
Taking with it His head, smiling still,
My wife screamed, terrifying and shrill,
God's Man had come to complete my Scheme,
Your scream was now mine, no time to dream.....

THIS . IS . THE . END

begun 2nd June 1984   *finish 19th February 1992*

Strangers in Parody

Nabil Shaban 1996

Gently Does It

Down in the basement, my friend and me,
Waiting to be killed, what misery,
It ain't normally what we relish,
With the stagnant air getting hellish,
Perculating round dusty sofas,
Our fear's driven by smiling chauffeurs.

My friend is trembling, he needs the loo,
His white eyes cry "Just say it ain't true,"
As I pity him, my anger grows,
Why must they kill us? God only knows,
Who gave them the right to load our dice?
Must we be meek lambs for sacrifice?

Just two of them, coming to end us,
Civil servant types, they want no fuss,
They have nice clean suits, they don't play games,
They won't even want to know our names,
And I doubt they know why we must die,
Just Grim Reapers that money can't buy.

I guess it began one April night,
My friend came to stay, the chat was light,
The topic was, how the world might end,
When the phone rang, it startled mv friend,
I picked it up but no sound came back,
So we joked about those Men in Black.

Two days later, my friend came again,
To plan the day should the Dark Lord reign,
Then, on cue, same time, the damn phone rang,
And a man whispered "Now you will hang."
Need I say I felt chilled to the bone,
But I braved a grin and licked the phone.

Three days on, 'bout one in the morning,
When driving home, my bells knelled warning,
Yellow headlamps menace behind me,
Could be yobs who kick Britain tidy,
Or more sinister, the Men in Black,
Either way, I hate them on my track.

I'd gone twenty miles up the road,
They still clung to me like debts were owed,
Then the fog swamped down to add some ache,
With luck those creeps would now overtake,
But no, even with my speed down low,
They hang right behind like sheep in tow.

I went even slower, they did too,
Which convinced me that my fears were true,
I must lose them before I reach home,
So killed my lights and while lost in foam,
I took the next side road on the right,
Which set me free and out of their sight.

But morning found my winnings were mean,
Some one sprayed blood on my car windscreen,
Warning me that I cannot escape,
Life in Death Row and Kafka's red tape,
So now we play patients waiting doom,
But my will is burning out this womb.

Why should I die for knowing too much?
Powers resent my being in touch, .
Dreams of spaceships heralding the end,
Drove me and my friend around the bend,
Evil regimes are taking control,
Global schemes for carving up the soul.

The visions are coming, thick and fast,
Love and peace are flowers decayeds past,
Ufos are hurtling against the wall,
Wedding cake shaped clouds echo the call,
But no one cares or pays attention,
There are things they won't let you mention.

They preach Greed is Good, let dog eat dog,
Get off my patch, I'm the best road-hog,
The poor must starve to prop up the rich,
Since might is right, fry the weak in pitch,
Sound-bites designed to hinder free-thought,
Right to guestion is easily bought.

The Church is God but the Spirit is not,
It's what we say counts, not what we got,
"Read my lips" means I'm telling the truth,
The Fruit of the Tree's no longer proof,
And that's why they want the Tree to die,
'Coz a smoked-screen sky hides Adam's lie.

Now we must pay for thinking this way,
And for seeing flying saucers play,
I've seen them five times, my friend just three,
But he dreamt he saw one circling me,
Then he saw Christ fly down with some more,
To save the poor from nuclear war.

I had a dream which hinted different,
There's no cavalry that's heaven sent,
Depend on no God for your rescue,
The answer's on Earth, it's up to you,
Priests and their rulers use yarns to bind,
Your strength to problems that they've defined,

In this dream I was in hospital,
A patient or staff, sane or mental?
Don't know, but I was trapped with the staff,
By a crazed mob who had the last laugh,
We locked the room to escape their wrath,
They'd had enough of being told off.

Behind barricades we tried to hide,
And ride the storm which could soon subside,
But no luck, outside the rampage grows,
If the walls break, it's our blood that flows,
As things grow worse, some suggested guns,
But I said "No, they're not solutions".

If I alone went out to see them,
A sacrifice might stop the mayhem,
The cowards agreed, so out I run,
My only weapon was compasion,
This passive approach blew out the flames,
And I left the two sides playing games.

The Price of Knowing Too Much

Nabil Shaban   2004

And since that dream happily rested,
Proving that Fate can be contested,
Why should I accept the death sentence,
Of faceless men who escapes conscience,
A surging edge says defend thyself,
Raise that cut-throat razor from the shelf.

My plan is to hide the flip-flap blade,
Beneath some blankets my mother made,
When the cardboard killer grips my throat,
I'll slash his wrists red and sink his boat,
A drastic tactic that contradicts,
How I pacified those lunatics.

As the clock struck eight my pal's pants reaked,
His nerves worm raped and his bowels had leaked,
His groans strive to keep Jesus alive,
When the Abysmal Exit Crew arrive,
Like bank managers nicking your bread,
Their lips kill Time when nothing is said.

The first one helped my friend to a chair,
And wrapped my towel round his neck with care,
As the poor lad was being throttled,
His brown eyes bulged like pickles bottled,
The second assassin held my head,
As my knife hand itched to slit him dead.

But this man's face said "I am your Dad."
"If you die by me, you will be glad."
He looked like a man who loved his wife,
Played with his kids, led a decent life,
His charm unhinged me, I begged reprieve,
That I could win was hard to believe.

Our moments of doubt are all they need,
To strangle our lives with their sly weed,
But what's the point of knowing this now,
 As he breaks my back for my last bow,
With pain fading to the dark within,
My mind is slipping the chains of sin.

29th February 1992.

Assassinating the Sixties Spirit of Freedom

Nabil Shaban 1981

The U. S. of Aids.

I am no journalist, and I aint no Private Dick,
I just yearn to sniff out things that oughtta make you sick,
Don't be fooled by my wheelchair, I'm someone they can't scare,
The story I have to tell you is all about AIDS,
Armaggeddon plague, a weapon man-made in the States,
If by the time you read this, it is known I am dead,
They'll have cooked up lies of suicide which you'll be fed.

One Sunday in Nineteen Eighty I read a chilling quote,
In the Observer, the triumph of the Reagan vote
Gave the Moral Majority "nuts" reason to gloat,
"Now, all Gays will be wiped out within a generation.."
What do they mean? What do they'know? Have they the means?
Has the New Right a secret plan of annihilation?
Bringing American Nazi world domination?

Then in May Eighty-One before Aids was all the rage,
I had this dream about an L-shaped virus rampage,
It began at the testicles and destroyed men's brains,
But women with exploding wombs and menstrual stains,
I witnessed first to fall screaming, then dead in the street.

The one man who knew died after he begged me to speak,
Alone in the summer snow blizzards, my task was bleak,
To warn the world of this new unstoppable disease,
That will destroy civilisation and end our species.

I must make a persuasive speech but I don't know how,
The Speech Writing Centre was closed with a big queue now,
As my panic grew, help came in the shape of my friend,
Who promised much but did nowt but drink tea in the end,
As my mind sank into the drifting waves of failure
I awoke from the dream, sensing a future foretold.

When Aids hit the headlines, I knew lies were being told,
A kinky black, in Africa, with a monkey was bold?
A punishment for sodomy sent from Doctor God?
Coming with the Far Right rise, aint it all rather odd?

Biological warfare was not new to the West
From Anthrax Island to enhanced Malarial pests,
Britain with it's Porton Down helped "friendly" forces with tests,
Chemicals and plagues are special "aids" in the genocide craze,
Churchill planned to gas Arabs if they refused to mend their ways,
White Rhodesians planted germs on freedom fighting blacks,
Trees and Vietnamese suffered "Agent Orange" attacks,
The C.I.A. used L.S.D. to render people weird,
And waged chemical warfare on Fidel Castro's beard.

Blue News Day: A Comic Relief

Nabil Shaban 1975

In Eighty-Three I wrote a treatise to stop the rot,
To warn the world that Aids was a C.I.A. plot,
And sent copies anonymously to embassies,
Journalists and politicians and TV grandees,
Because it wouldn't do, if my hunch and thinking was true,
For the Aids-makers to know my name, and thus who to do,
Nothing changed in Eighty Four, so I sent out some more.

When I told my friends my theory, most thought I was mad,
The Last Great Conspiracy Freak, something rather sad,
As the Hidden Fascists spread their spite, my heart felt low,
Then one day I heard on Spike Milligan's T.V. show,
A radio D.J. say some think Aids was Lab-Made,
And repeated in a drama the BBC played,
Entitled "...And Here is the News." by G.F.Neuman.

Then I saw Channel Four prove in a telly programme,
The claim that Africa's to blame was a total sham,
And disinformation had made monkeys of us all,
Some biologists maintained some boffins had a ball
Creating the Aids agent by splicing retroviruses,
Helping the Yank government to commit greater piracies.
Bit by bit my instinct was being vindicated.

The question is why, they have gone to all this trouble?
Re-assert God's lore which had long since burst its bubble?
The Sixties helped make the Right to Question a virtue,
Those fake Victorian values exist to hurt you
Repression thrives on an atmosphere of fear,
Our Rulers need signs to suggest God's wrath is near
Religion sustains tha authority of the state,
Convenient Aids provides well-timed targets to hate.

You think you have problems when Mad Mullahs run the state,
What if Christian Amaggedonists govern your fate?
The Book of Revelations makes a blood-thirsty read,
Two thirds must be sacrificed when Christ King comes to lead,
If this is desired by the most powerful nation,
Whose science can make flesh, prophets' imagination,
And when Bible-Punchers own the Presidential ear,
And if you're not WASP, you've got one helluva lot to fear.

Live Aids in Africa is much more than a sick joke,
Besides the hated Gays, they've got it in for black folk,
Humankind must be cleansed of racial impurities,
The growing Coloured Poor threaten White Supremacists,
To dare to take what's theirs, invites western nemesis.

The Eggman Cometh   Nabil Shaban 1983

The U.S. has five percent of world population,
Consumes over half what the Earth's able to ration,
And add their Euro lap-dogs who gobble yet a third,
Which leaves for the globe's four-fifth, an amount that's absurd,
With such unequal shares, there'll never be any peace,
New weapons are needed to aid the non-whites' decrease,
Which keeps the environment intact for Northern greed,
With no competition, their affluence can't recede.

Perhaps I'm too quick to assert sinister motives,
Dread of revenge is why it's fiction the guilty gives,
Maybe just an experiment that went rather wrong,
And was unwittingly let loose amidst Afric's throng,
Concocted killer virus by chance pollutes vaccine,
Whichever way you choose it, the story's still obscene.

Recently the Post brought facts that help support my case,
In Nineteen Seventy, the U.S. gave funds to chase
The goal of synthetic biological agents,
Designed with a racial or ethnic specifity,
Which won't exist in nature, for which there's no defense
Via an acquired natural immunity,
That could decimate an enemy community.
WHO in Seventy-two offered to tip the waiter,
So ten million dollars and seven years later,
A new bio-weapon of mass destruction was born,
In the fires of Forts Dettrick and Meade glowed Gallo's dawn.

H.I.V. parents are pretty well identified,
The Bovine Leukemia Virus forced to ride,
The cancer-causing Sheep Visna, sad Mother of Aids,
And spawned the virile viral master of T-cell raids.

Thus a program of Aids-laced smallpox vaccination,
Sent in Seventy-Seven for the blacks nation,
New World ethnic weapon aimed at de-population,
While in Seventy-Eight "Operation Trojan Horse"
A scheme the Moral Majority were to endorse,
Arranged for over two thousand American Gays,
To be injected with laced Hepatitus B stays.

If my dream painted the Aids-ridden picture to come,
Then was the "L" in the L-shaped virus not so dumb?
A clue suggesting a Laboratory-shaped bio-bomb,
Was the "L" describing much more than the shape of Hell?
Perhaps hinting at words like "Leukemia" as well,
Maybe "Lentivirus", "Lymphotropic" or "Lysing",
Dream of Tropic of Cancer with a Bad Moon Rising.

The Fascist Backlash   Nabil Shaban 1983

By Eighty-Nine, there were five million Aids cases,
And doubling every year, soon no safe oasis,
By Ninety-six, three-quarters of us will be dead,
Leaving year Two Thousand and One, a dream dulled to lead.
This according to a John Lear is the Grand Culling Plan,
The virus will be stopped when a quarter remains of Man,
He claims the United States government has got the cure,
But will not use it until the New Order is secure.

Don't think Safe Sex will save you, the Condom is a con,
The rubbers are riddled with holes that enlarge when on,
With the smallest, at least twice the size of the Aids poop,
So it's like shooting golf balls through a basketball hoop.
You can catch this vile virion without having sex,
Saliva can hasten you from this world to the next,
Aids-infected blood to mosquitoes is just as nice,
As it is no less tasty to bed bugs and head lice.

As usual, those who have attempted to spill the beans,
Are now silent behind bars or plugged by other means,
Raymond Manchester, a Yank driver in the army,
Chanced upon tapes and documents which drove him barmy,
They detailed how H.I.V. had been designed and made,
With plans, for introducing it into nations, laid,
Giving proof this was brewed under Gallo's supervision
And now Mister Manchester is rotting in prison.

Doctor Robert Strecker and his lawyer brother Ted,
Discovered corroborations and now his brother's dead,
They made it look like Ted had shot himself in the head,
Next to go was Chicago Congressman Douglas Huff,
When he backed Strecker's facts, the Nasties had to play rough,
He was a damn nuisance on radio and T.V.
So he was "suicided" by Smack and Coke O.D.

Those who still attempt to expose the Aids cover up,
Suffer death threats, phone taps and cars with their brakes fucked up.

Don't expect the truth from governments, experts and media,
They refuse to confess for fear of public hysteria,
Confidence in the integrity of Science and State,
Would melt into despair and revive as blood-curdling hate.

Perhaps we just have to face it, we're a race of shit,
If Aids does wipe us out, quite frankly we deserve it,
Our consciousness hasn't stopped us from being vicious and greedy
Unless it's in our interests we happily forsake the needy
We suck the planet dry, and give nothing in return,
Man is his own self-destruct button, destined to burn,
So when he gets too big for his boots, he'll put himself to sleep,
And when he finally does, neither Nature nor I will weep.

11th April 1992

The Cardiologists

Nabil Shaban 1974

WHAT DOES IT COST A MAN.
Owed (Ode?) to Anarchy.

The silver fish are spinning in dustbin circles,
Hearing weird sounds beat echo races anyday,
To a stake my name was born tied with local cords,
Drift wide and far on a partial severance pay,
Til the high blade beckons to cut what gloss remains,
 And with no grammar I'll be free,
To hook Lost Chords on Anarchy.

Moist orgasmic ruptures suck honey-lit shudders,
Universally desired for it's sweetened pain,
That explodes in swift densities of fires,
Beholden to nought but a dream container brain,
Self-played pleasuring help make islands of us all,
Lust's a prison spelt fantasy,
Love's a God spreading Anarchy.

Hire a sea horse. Coz they're laughing at the starving.
I was. He was. I was carving. He was carving.
I was carving a dollar whilest He carved my mind.
I gave him my dollar in exchange for what's mine.
The shame of the Shaver piles blame on my craving,
Money should plead insanity,
And hit the notes in Anarchy.

Absurd is the door to the imagination
Caterpillars die never knowing butterflies,
Sad loathing of a feared corpse denies creation,
Common sense says angels from men are utter lies,
Grisly crysalis is freedom's ugly foreplay,
Screen unseen hides the Shaman's key,
Body lies still for Anarchy.

Crumbling certainties makes molehills out of mountains,
Bleeding gums recede presenting empty mouthings,
Joints and wrists scream for cool hedonistic fountains,
When kettles feel. heavy, expect no more outings,
Days and nights plagued with chest and head in arrears,
Time is life's ruthless allergy,
The only cure is Anarchy.

Too Late Too Soon, The Final Cull-mination

Nabil Shaban 1981

Crowds saw clouds assume the guise of shroud wrapped mushrooms,
Pain breaks the dreamless sleep that drowns in fetid fear,
Thunder in the afternoon nurtures nerves for tombs,
Space and time bates at the apex of the dropped tear,
Tangle of coincidences build nests of doom,
Please choose your prophet cannily,
As Fate belongs to Anarchy.

The morning woke me stabbing panic in my head,
Numb little fingers on the left hand looking blue,
A sudden burst of nowhere music wants me dead,
Vice-like feelings try to draw me up through the roof,
Paralysing loss of consciousness spreads like lead,
The Will to live is vanity,
Soften Death's grip with Anarchy.

Waiting for the clock is like dripping on the spot,
Wasting crazy hours with a mug of day-dream tea,
Paintings that unwind in a mind that loves to rot,
Never disappointing if no fruit on the tree,
The unwritten novel can never betray me,
Purity is salutory,
If left to live with Anarchy.

Be not surprised by my unexpected demise,
Every lonely death is a nail in my coffin,
When the world tires of life, the stars will always rise,
There is no sadness when atoms do the shopping,
Only consequences with memories for eyes,
All existence is agony,
Unless you cheat with Anarchy.

A spot on the ceiling is ringing in my ears,
As when all else fades to the haze of stagnant hues,
The veneer of silence promotes whispers to cheers,
And thoughts that refuse to choose are ones that you lose,
Brave the blank slate of awareness punctured with spears,
The enemy is flattery,
Let Ego die for Anarchy.

16th April 1992.

Inner Space   Nabil Shaban 2001

NUMBERS OF THE BEAST.

It's crazy but true Numbers build an Ark Two by Two,
Accept Black is White, One is All, Heaven is Hell,
Nay is Yea, the Jewel is the Crown, the Square is Round,
Everything is Opposite, what you Lose can be Found,
The Ring is a Spiral, Winter is Summer, War is a Whore,
Destruction is Creation, the Assassin is Messiah,
The Apocalypse is Salvation, the Dream is a Nightmare.

The Meaning is in the Sums, Order means Nothing,
The Numbers say Ugly is Beauty, so you mustn't cry,
We should count the beasts who steal fruit from your eye.

Alien from Sirius begets its Dragon,
Satan cracked an Egg with a Stone called Adam,
The End of the Circle is both Open and Shut,
Meaning the Snake is Eve and the Lock is the Key,
The Core of the Apple makes the Pip your Home.

If the Spelling can ride High, then the Numbers don't Lie,
Seasoning of Reason creates a Style of Why,
He's a Devil of a Beast, taking Fruit from his Eye

Take Christ from Positive, be left with Negative,
Take Jesus from Love and be left with Hate,
Fluid is Solid with Energy added,
Jesus was a Comet, an Omen for Change,
Death will Light your Fire on the Cross of Time.

If the Spelling can ride High, then the Numbers don't Lie,
Seasoning of Reason creates a Style of Why,
He's a Devil of a Beast, taking Fruit from his Eye

From Nowhere the Mother is a Door to the Earth,
The Answer is a Mystery when the Question is Forgotten,
The Word is Knowledge meaning Truth Is Destiny,
Life is Good, Fear is Evil, God is Unity.

If the Spelling can ride High, then the Numbers don't Lie,
Seasoning of Reason creates a Style of Why,
He's a Devil of a Beast, taking Fruit from his Eye

Know that the Secret Chiefs are The Nine Unknown Men,
The same as the Old Ones who know your Best Friend,
Who is both Guardian and Angel from the Abyss,
The Stranger, the Outsider with the Hidden Kiss.

The Green Mania   Nabil Shaban   1999

If the Spelling can ride High, then the Numbers don't Lie,
Seasoning of Reason creates a Style of Why,
He's a Devil of a Beast, taking Fruit from his Eye

The Sun is Red, the Moon is Blood,
Jesus is the Bride, Mary is Bread,
Christ is the Groom, the Fish is Wine,
At the Wake most Weep, some Laugh while others Smile,
Add Resurrection to Crucifixion, you have the Holy Grail..

If the Spelling can ride High, then the Numbers don't Lie,
Seasoning of Reason creates a Style of Why,
He's a Devil of a Beast, taking Fruit from his Eye

Liberty is the Sacrifice of the Spirit,
Swapping Chaos for a Body that is Prison.
If Iron that's Yellow accepts Paper that's Gold
Equality is a Legend the Will must Rule.
The Bible is Freedom but it's also a Myth,
Claiming Charity and Peace is no Illusion.

The Abacus played with Napier's Bones spat a Numeral,
My albatross strayed to salvage a home at a funeral.

The Mind thinks it's Way to the Soul through Alchemy,
From Water to Silver, Harmony shines Surreal.
The Power as Glory will Help call Omega,
To End the Fun and Virtue of all Existence.
If Desire is a Sin, then Justice is a Ghost,
Like the Trickster who plays Saviour in a Ufo.

Confucius Computes the cowardly Cipher of dry Letters,
The obstruse refutes the hourly writers of my betters.

Mass craves Anarchy which the Heart makes Posslble,
Through the Crucible of Chance and Revolution.
Religion is a Game whose Goal is a Mirage,
From Womb to Grave, Faith is a Chain of Confuslon.
Reality is Law but then Physics is a Fox,
Your journey to Know will Progress to Delusion.

What maketh the Words worth their Summation is the smaller Whole,
Hot acres of burnt earth scare some nation to play the cheap role.

6th May 1992

Help Me

Nabil Shaban 1998

<u>Welcome Back, Jesus, your Cell is still Warm</u>

Ah, Jesus, welcome home.
Come and meet your new friends,
We are all called Christ here
Please, don't think we are mad,
We make up the many,
The ones that don't believe,
Are few and quite insane.

So let's all smile as we hand out the nails,
And laugh as we ring a crown of thorns,
Smirk as we sip the sexy vinegar,
And joke heartily as we jab the spear.

Wine flows from our wounds as we piss blood,
Caviar drops from our arse as we puke excrement,
Dripping taps have more music than a Hollywood waterfall,
So go away and come back next Millenium,
When you've learnt your lines better,
 And won't drop your Martyr's props.

15th April 1995

Re-invention and Re-play of a Restless Atom   Nabil Shaban   2000

You're Nothing

There's nothing in this life that's not recycled vice,
There's not a thought in your head that's not yet been bought,
There's not a word that's bin said which aint been heard,
Every idea you had was another Joe's fad,
You ain't original, you've been had before,
Your hips aren't political, they've been swayed before,
If you fuck like Jesus, then your arse must be sore,
You're not the best that's ever been, cause that would be obscene,
It's a dirty old world that turns on graves,
A birth is nothing new,
It's just another sod from a fucked up screw.

20th April 1995

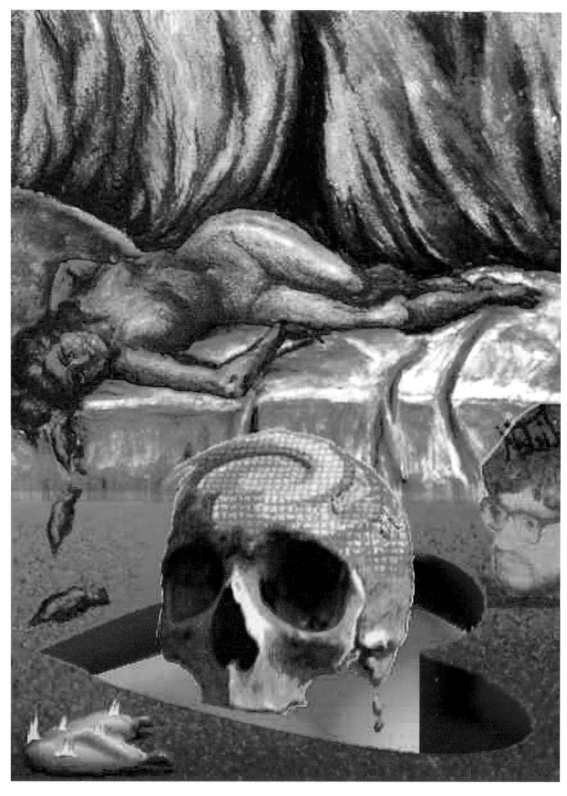

Head Over Heels   Nabil Shaban 1975

I never want....

I never want to say goodbye now,
I never want to bid you welcome,
I never caught that train anyhow,
It was the long and wrong way home.

chorus
I see the tremble in your handshake,
I see the dark smile on your Corn Flake,
I see the poison in your heart-ache,
And life is death to the rolling groan.

I never want to be your night-lite,
I never want to be love's cell-mate,
I never want the blame when we fight,
It was the long and wrong way home.

chorus
I see the tremble..... etc

I never want to climb your stairway,
I never want to fall from your grace,
I never want say what you say,
It was the long and wrong way home.

I taste the grief on your bitter lips,
I hear the sigh of ten sunken ships,
I smell the blood on bad judges' whips,
And time will shake the dust from our bones.

26th June 1996

Seconds before the....Shhhh, mustn't tell anyone   Nabil Shaban 1987

Impulse

You'll never get there,
Don't drive on your own,
You're very reckless,
Please don't die alone.

The journey's far,
The journey's wide,
You've never been to the other side,
It's a town of a million debts,
Multiplied by your life's regrets.

So please don't be brave,
Put away that knife,
It's only a book,
When it's not my life.

1st July 1996

OM Sweet OM

Nabil Shaban 2002

What is...... But....

What is great on the inside,
But small on the outside?
What is superior within,
But nonessential without?
What is a private beauty,
But a public deformity?
What has a wise interior,
But a foolish exterior?
An inner Omnipresence,
But an outer finality?
What is secretly awake,
Yet apparently asleep......
         ....The God in You.

1st July 1996

Another Sky that Keeps Falling   Nabil Shaban 1999

Rewind the Fast-forward

Out of Time, came Light and Dark,
A clash of gods' startling spark,
    From the crash of fire and ice,
Good and Bad danced to entice.

Swirling themes and dreams foretold,
By stones, trees and stars of old,
    She and He in turn control
Nature's spinning parasol.

With Give and Take, Love and Hate,
Over-ruled to alternate,
    Life forces a division,
Giving Death the decision.

4th July 1996

Anti-podium Self - Portrait

Nabil Shaban 1999

The Rag Doll

Please, darling, don't you take me…..
                          …….for something that I'm not,
And don't you take from me….
                          ……what little faith I've got,
    And don't you break me….
                          …….into a million drowning dots,
                    Because my heart is not….
…a Ferris Wheel of Love.

22nd July 1996

The Transmigration of Souls and the Recycling of Spiritual Waste   Nabil Shaban 1976

Heady Stuff

The tilting candle tips,
The larva flow of waste,
Which hardens into bricks,
To fall in blood - red space.

From the echoes of doom,
Charge a train of faces,
Road raging dolled up tunes,
Inside laughing sages.

The flame - cooled Triangle,
Gives voice to a pipe-dream,
Dripping drops of candle,
To quench the mood yer in.

As the spheres coalesce,
Into bugs of fear,
Your journey comes to rest,
When your skin is weird.

2nd Aug. 1996

The Time is NOW

Nabil Shaban 1980

Earl Grey

So you want to meet an alien and you want to fly high?
    Earl Grey, let the space in,
And you're bored with all this world but you never want to die,
    Earl Grey, let the space in.

And you dream of Christ in a space-ship who will save this earth,
    Earl Grey, let the space in,
But we're just the Watchers and we're here for the mirth,
    Earl Grey, let the space in.

You've enough aliens in your own world, who are despised by you,
    Earl Grey, let the space in,
When you learn to love them, then maybe E.T. will love you too.
    Earl Grey, let the space in.

14th Aug. 1996

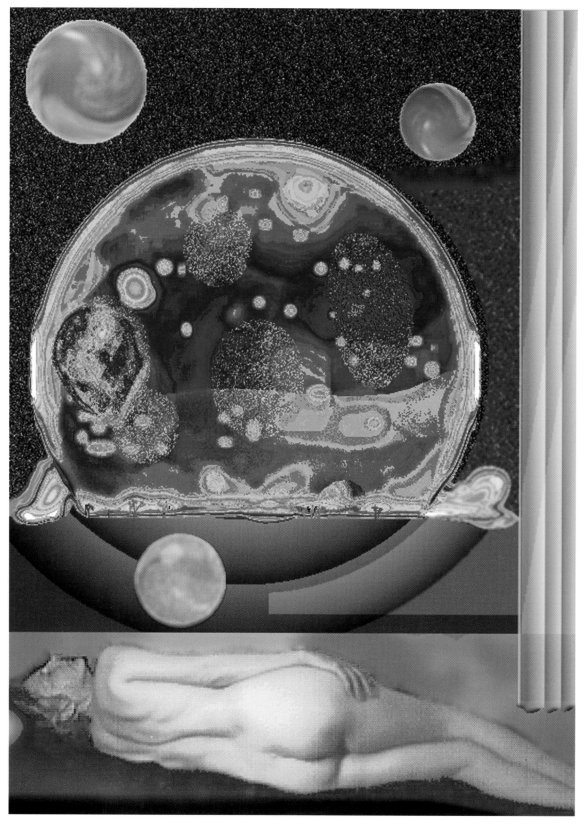

Waiting for Gaia   Nabil Shaban 1998

<u>Quickly Heaven Passes</u>

The Silence was screaming with expectation,
You took me up Passion's Hill,
The still white stars above, smile on their orange sisters below,
As they paint a dreaming city,
Oblivious of the two birds rising from the ashes as one,
A fox ambles past, looks back and nods her approval,
We have no more words, only feelings,
In shy desire I take your hand,
And you reward me with a consuming embrace,
Filled with kisses that melt me into your very being,
If Eternity is this sweet, then let us die now.

17th Oct. 1996

The First to Go   Nabil Shaban 1998

Hitler is Not Dead

When a Deaf friend of mine tells me - doctors in the Seventies,
secretly tried to sterilize him,
then I know we have been lied to - Hitler is not Dead

When a Disabled friend tells me she will be denied child benefit
if she refuses to abort her disabled child,
then I know we have been lied to - Hitler is not Dead

When I read in Hansard that the ex-Thatcherite regime made it legal
to kill Disabled foetuses that have achieved full term,
then I know we have been lied to - Hitler is not Dead

When I read in the newspapers Neo-Nazis escape the Penalty of the Law,
when burning down a home for disabled people,
then I know we have been lied to - Hitler is not Dead

When I see on TV that a British doctor has murdered a Disabled kid,
by depriving it of food, drink and medication,
then I know we have been lied to - Hitler is not Dead

When I hear a Genetic Scientist proudly proclaim
he wants to create the Perfect Baby,
then I know we have been lied to - Hitler is not Dead

6th February 1998

The Sleeping Continent

Nabil Shaban 1999

Touched

The silky hand of Leanne,
Soothes the brow of the savage beast,
Combing the land in search of sand,
To build a castle for a sleeping Queen,
Lost in a creepy dream,
Full of wandering trees,
With nothing to eat but cheese.

The heavy hand of Leanne,
Grasps a rod of iron to brand,
The faithless heart of a man,
Who erects Towers of Flowers,
To Love timed in golden hours,
And leaves her soul wasted,
On a bleak beach that's beyond reach.

23 February 1998

What the Vicar refused to tell me   Nabil Shaban 1974

Tall Story

What is there left to love,
With no heaven above?
All the doves have been killed,
The cemeteries filled,
Cupid's bow is broken,
Romance a mere token,
The stupid crow croaks
All the world's a phase
Rejoice, we're sinking,
The dumb telly jokes
All life is a maze,
We'll do your thinking.

24th February 1998

Sharon The Ferry Queen

Nabil Shaban 1996

<u>Carrowkeel</u>

We'll meet at half-past seven,
Pass through the Gate of Heaven,
And I'll be clean for the Faerie Queen,
But when the Changeling's return is seen,
Perhaps the Fey Ones won't be so keen,
And thus hide from my now mortal eyes,
The Key to unlock Sidhe Paradise.

11th May 1998

Sil-eeeeeee Bugger

Nabil Shaban 2004

Alienation

I do not like my body,
Never have, it's so shoddy,
It has always been my Enemy,
Stopping me from being me,
It won't let me walk and it won't let me run,
Always trying to stop me from having fun,
"Be careful. You'll break a bone", grown-ups would say,
Keeping me still, and away from kids at play,
Not many girls will want a boy like me,
So I think I'll hide in the highest tree,
But I can't, coz I can't climb,
Damn and blast this body of mine,

Yeah, well, it ain't gonna defeat me,
My stubbornness that I'll never sell,
I'll get to the top of the mountain,
With or without this Body from Hell.

24th May 1998

The Fish That Got Away   Nabil Shaban 1998

<u>To the Goddess Ancestor of Ireland</u>

My darling sweet Dana,
Are you a pirahna?
If I swim in your sea,
Will you come and eat me?

She beckons me with her hips,
From her soft, sinful lips,
She replies with a sigh,
"There are worse ways to die!"

20th July 1998

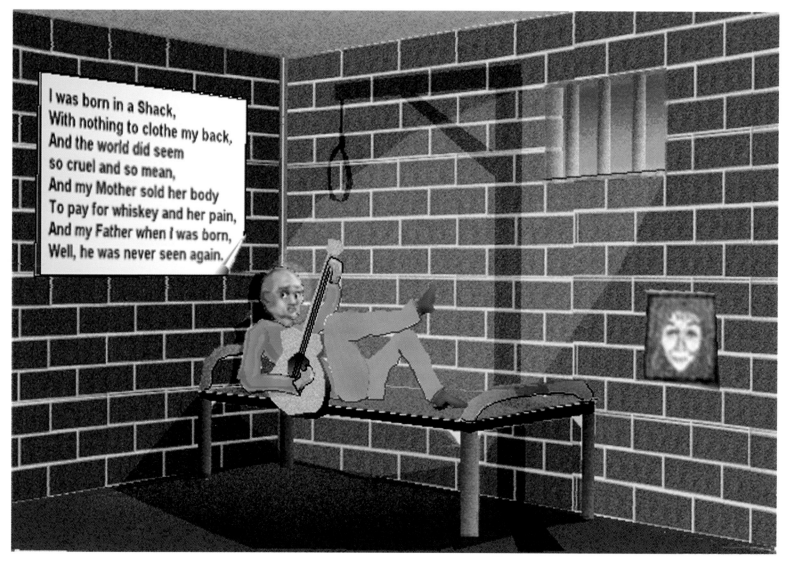

I've Got the Tired Old Cliché Blues

Nabil Shaban 1999

The Essential Blues Song

I was born in a shack,
With nothing to clothe my back,
And the world did seem
 so cruel and so mean,
And my Mother, she sold her body
To pay for whiskey and her pain,
And my Father when I was born,
Well, he was never seen again.

6th June 1999

117

Aphrodite wishing she was in a Dali painting   Nabil Shaban 1984

The Rock of Deludia

When the heaven blessed stars bedazzle the pitch black skies
I see the sparkling shine of your lovely warm brown eyes

When the raven's ebony wings fly past snowy clouds that roll and billow
I see your long silky dark midnight hair embrace my gleaming white pillow

When I see your smile, it puts my head in a spin
Your number I dial makes me cry if you're not in

Deludiah, I am no farmer, but let me plough your field
And between us, plant sweet dreams of Love's perfect yield

I am your fiery Tiger, and you're my dancing Dolphin
Dare to tame my claws of passion with your baby doll-like fin

And between the jungle and the sea
Our eternal love will roam wild and free

Let us look forward to the day, when we finally go away
To my Skyland where the stars stay, giving our love the chance to play

Let us trust each other with our hearts, bodies and souls
Flying to the sun with light, peace and fun as our goals

8th May 2000

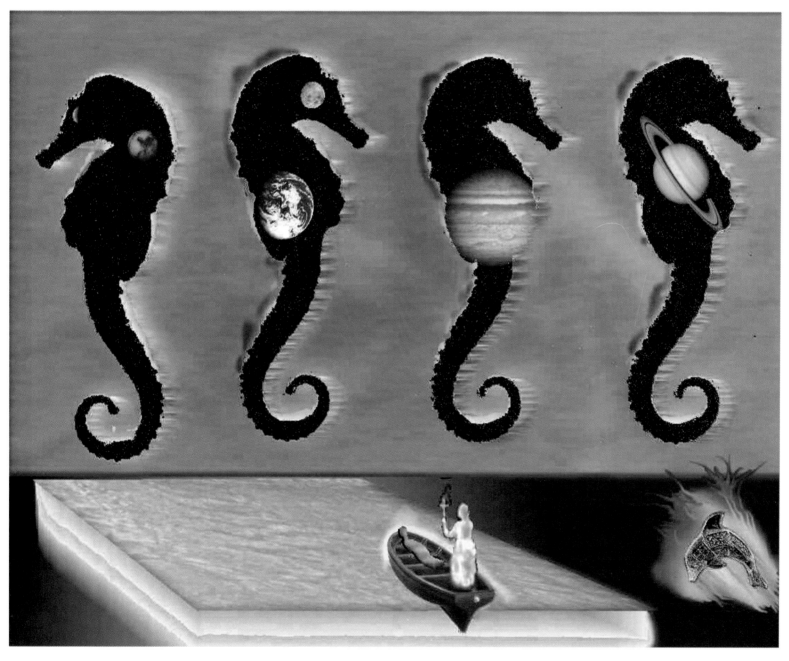

Sharon The Ferry Queen Never Rests   Nabil Shaban 2002

Her Heart is like an Ocean

Tina Teenager, Teen at Heart,
Gone forty now, don't fall apart,
Child of fire, flames kept you bright,
Burning anger disrupts the night,
Motherless child - Mother to All,
Pain you suffer unmasks God's call,
Fairies beckon, piping sweet tunes,
Flowers unfold like mystic runes,
Rainbow fish gives colour to blue,
Man's world of hate is not for you,
Don't die screaming your life was worthless,
Survive this nightmare and pass the Test.

29th July 2000

Chickens that Come Home to Roost

Nabil Shaban 1975

War of the Worlds   (or   The Soldier's Lament)

When I got home, the war had taken its toll
The house was in ruins, all was black as coal
Charred shadows of wife and babe etched on the floor
On seeing her ghost, my tears did implore....

"Why did you go without me? Why did you go without me?"
My love shook her head and said
Words that should have struck me dead

"You left me alone in this world of despair,
Forsaken, lost in an alien nightmare,
Besieged in our home, abandoned to my fate,
I died waiting for you at the garden gate."

"Why did you go without me? Why did you go without me?"
My love shook her head and said
Words that should have struck me dead

"I cried "Where are you?" when they smashed down my door,
Our baby they slew, a martyr to your war,
You said you would be gone for just a few days,
Now we've been fried by ultra-violent rays."

"Why did you go without me? Why did you go without me?"
My love shook her head and said
Words that should have struck me dead

"Everything has gone, all that you hold dear,
Our dreams stolen in cargoes of fear,
Is life worthless, now emptied of our love?
Forever your cries shall scream to Those above....."

"Why did I go without them? Why did I go without them?"

23rd February 2001

The Final Curtain Call   Nabil Shaban 1999

Such a Silly Walrus called….John

Hey John, you should have just played music for fun,
You should never have tried to move the world on,
Whoa John! You got yourself shot, you stupid moron,
Is that the only way to end your song?
Oh you are such a silly, silly boy…called John.

Oh John, where did all you hippies go wrong?
Those flowers blowing in the wind have bloody well gone,
Sixties' Love and Peace was just a put on,
You died because someone thought you was such a con,
Oh you silly, silly-billy boy…called John.

John, did you have to be totally in love with death?
John, did you have to leave us so utterly bereft?
John, have you reached Heaven, 'cause that's too far out for us?
John, does God agree you're more popular than Jesus?

We miss you, You silly silly boy…called John,
'Cause those arseholes have turned another War on.

27th April 2001
revised 9th December 2004

125

Bathing   Nabil Shaban 1986

A Halloween Fantasy

At last a dream is coming true
Shape of which is a girl that's you
Naughty brown bright eyes that tease
Long whispering black hair that flow with ease
Liquid lips that melt and silky tongue that soothes
Your smile keeps me still whilest everything moves
The sweetness of your charms warms my frosty heart
I love you, Fantana, don't ever let us part.

A happy day will come when we become one
Mind, body and soul union basking in the sun
An ocean of love merges two figures in stone
A blending of twin hopes into a shiny new home
Fantasia, light source of the stars
Faint Asia, Dream Queen of the mountain,
Fate Ayesa, Blue Lady of the lake,
Your gentle soul keeps my love awake.

31st October 2002

We are ALL Responsible

Nabil Shaban 2001

Emergency Call: History Murdered

You can't expect to fly with oil-soaked wings,
Beneath the Blair Smile Smirks His Tory Grin.
No, Don't be Conned,
Such a small fry
Dreaming of a big pond
That smarmy Erronyous Blagg
Is just a sad Thatcher in Drag,
Lets sell Britain to America
Lets all die on the Fourth of July

Who cares about the Ozone layer?
Air and water should never be free
You can demand a price if you create scarcity
So lets help those damn Yanks suck up your world
Virtual Dreams build sand castles around your head
And the TV dinners leave crumbs in your bed.
Oil burning land thrives on a clueless bush
Fuelling the Fool on Capital's Hill,
When the Rich want more, you can count on War
Bright video glass eyes shield towers of lies
In their campaign to make scapegoats of the Poor.

11th September 2003

Bubble of Hope

Nabil Shaban 1988

The Fire Horse

Queen of Mars, she stole my heart
Now I know we must never part
Through the snow she drives the sky cart
She is my exquisite love banquet
Life's cuisine squeezed in a rose bouquet
she's my stairway to the heavenly feast
I bury my face in her golden fleece
Comb her zones of intimate pleasures
Like an infant Drinking sweet nectar
from her cup of infinite treasures….
The more I rave crave for her
This Queen of Moravia,
Stramberk's revenge, never tasted sweeter
Nothing I can do that will defeat her
From her lips I relish the cream with which
she pacified the ancient Tartar sword
settling old scores with a different type of sauce
Tantalizingly tantric this ice Zena of Tatra Heights
I., that is dragon, wolf and leopard in one
Crumbled before she, the Martial swan
cloaked in the pearl white uniform
of the gentle innocent unicorn
Surrendering as her BramBora- potato
baked boiled mushed and mashed in a magic halo
Joyously pulped and vaporized by the fiery
fumes of the Garlician equinus love
It is true, not a saga, this proud princess of Praga
A golden gift born from the spark
of the ignacious encircling advance
upon this trembling Blue Earth by mirth's
Smiling passion Red Martian romance
Playfully attired as the fairy mermaid of eros
Spinning a shrinking orbital web
To net and return to her loving eternal embrace
Her soul's other half, the wandering cosmic twin
Like a tail-less lamb, lost and last in the human race
And now upon the carpet of blues, greens and reds reflected
in the rainbow spectrum celestial of physical, sexual, spiritual
An organic orgasmic expressive dance of atomic Precipitation,
Melts, melds and merges the sacred Venus and Mars re-unification.

31st December 2003